Fur or Fins

By Sally Cowan

Lots of things swim in the sea.

Some have fur and some
have fins.

Fish and whales have fins to help
them swim in the surf.

Seals swim in cold parts of the sea.

They need fur to keep the cold out.

fur

A fur seal dives deep
in chilly seas to get fish.

It has thick fur to keep
it snug.

Big fur seals swim out
and hunt fish.

Then they ride the surf back
to feed their pups.

A harp seal is born
with soft white fur.

It's cute and fluffy!

fur

Harp seal pups grow
and grow.

They shed their white fur.

Big harp seals have fur
with dark spots.

big seal

pup

Fur seals and harp seals
twist and turn
when they swim.

Then they curl up
on the beach for a nap.

Sharks do not have fur.

They have big fins that are long and stiff.

The fins help sharks swim.

fins

This shark lurks in the sea.

It waits for a fish
to swim by.

Then, it rushes and takes
a big bite!

Some sharks are very big.

This shark is named
a whale shark.

It can slurp up lots of fish
at once.

Whales have great big fins and a wide tail.

They can jump and turn and make a big splash.

Many other things with fur
swim in the sea, too!

And many others have fins!

fins

fur

CHECKING FOR MEANING

1. What are two words that the author uses to describe the harp seal? *(Literal)*

2. How does a whale shark eat? *(Literal)*

3. Why do you think fur seals do not take their pups hunting with them? *(Inferential)*

EXTENDING VOCABULARY

snug	How does it feel to be *snug*? Fur seals have thick fur to keep snug. How can you stay snug?
lurks	What does it mean if you *lurk* somewhere? What other word could the author have used instead of *lurks* in the sentence *This shark lurks in the sea.*?
slurp	*Slurp* is an example of a word that sounds like its meaning. Say the word slowly. How does this help you to understand what the word means?

MOVING BEYOND THE TEXT

1. What is your favourite animal with fins? Why do you like it?

2. What do you think the fur on a fur seal feels like to touch?

3. What other animals with fur can you think of that swim in the sea?

4. Would you rather have fur or fins? Why?

SPEED SOUNDS

ar	er	ir	ur	or

PRACTICE WORDS

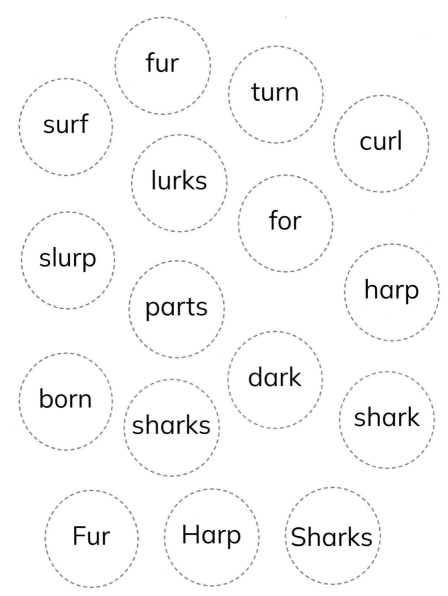

fur

turn

surf

curl

lurks

for

slurp

harp

parts

born

dark

sharks

shark

Fur

Harp

Sharks